The Country in Her Throat

The Country In Her Throat

SIMON FORTIN
TRANSLATED BY
BILL GLASSCO

The Country in Her Throat
first published 1994 by
Scirocco Drama
An imprint of J. Gordon Shillingford Publishing Inc.
© Copyright Simon Fortin, 1992
English Translation © Copyright Bill Glassco, 1994

Cover design by Terry Gallagher/Doowah Design
Cover photo courtesy of the School of Contemporary Dancer's
Translator's photo by Michel Boulianne
Printed and bound in Canada by Hignell Printing Ltd.

Published with the generous assistance of The Canada Council.

Canadian Cataloguing in Publication Data

Fortin, Simon, 1961-
The country in her throat

A play.
ISBN 1-896239-01-3

I. Title.
PS8561.O77C68 1995 C842'.54   C95-910264-7
PQ3919.2.F67C68 1995

For Marie Gignac, my actress of silences, her are some words to fill up your mouth.
And, as always, for Paul Browde

Author's Note

As a child, I used to daydream at my father's bookshelves, inventing the content of books I hadn't yet read, wondering if this story or that story would satisfy my curiosity. I resisted *Forty Years of Song*, Emma Albani's autobiography, for quite a long time. On ultimately reading it, my resistance was validated. It was intensely disappointing.

What did fascinate me, however, lay in what was not said, what was obviously omitted or obsequiously embellished. Not so much the sure-to-be-found mud under her shiny shoes, but the apparent shallowness of a famous artist's life turned into avuncular prose. Ghostwritten, I immediately thought! As a matter of fact, I was wrong. She wrote it.

But I was left with the feeling she hadn't necessarily lived what was written. I then took it upon myself to fill in the gaps of silence and was left facing those who listened to her, those who held the ladder, those who shared her long journey into exile for the sake of Art. Therefore this is my story of Emma Albani, told through their silence.

I believe our lives are given to us by those who listen to us, those who stand in the wings of our existence. I believe our lives are the expression of a long quest to be listened to. It is certainly true of an opera singer's life. Thus, it makes sense to say that we all lead ghostwritten lives. My first play is about these ghosts. Hers. And I still daydream in front of bookshelves.

Simon Fortin

Production Credits

The Country In Her Throat premiered on May 18, 1994, at the Tarragon Theatre, Toronto, Canada, with the following cast:

EMMA ALBANI LAJEUNESSE ....Lally Cadeau
CORNELIA LAJEUNESSE ....Clare Coulter
EVA ....Moira Young
FREDERIC/ERNEST GYE ....Benedict Campbell
QUEEN VICTORIA ....Frances Hyland

Directed by Bill Glassco
Musical Direction by Elizabeth Acker
Set and Costumes designed by John Ferguson
Lighting designed by Paul Mathieson
Stage Manager: Susan Monis

Note: In this, as in the original production in French, the musical director was onstage throughout, playing a real piano.

Characters

EMMA ALBANI LAJEUNESSE, Soprano
CORNELIA LAJEUNESSE, her sister
EVA, a pupil
FREDERIC GYE, Director of Covent Garden
ERNEST GYE, his son
QUEEN VICTORIA

Note: the text in heavy type covers the singing lesson, whereas the text in regular type signifies a return to the past.

Music

"She is far from the Land" (Moore/Lambert)
"Ah! non credea mirarti" (Bellini, *La Sonnambula*)
"Qui la voce" (Bellini, *I Puritani*)
"Dove Sono" (Mozart, *The Marriage of Figaro*)
"Vissi d'arte, vissi amore" (Puccini, *Tosca*)
"Home Sweet Home" (Payne/Bishop)
"Connais-tu le pays?" (Thomas, *Mignon*)
"Ombra mai fu" (Handel, *Xerxes*)

Simon Fortin

Simon Fortin has been involved in theatre both as an actor
and a playwright, both in English and French Canada. His
other plays (co-authored with Guylaine Tremblay) include
Poison d'Avril and *Souriez Mille Robi*. He has also
written fiction and radio drama. He currently lives in New
York City.

Bill Glassco

Bill Glassco is the founding artistic director of Toronto's Tarragon Theatre, co-founding artistic director of the Canadian Stage Company, and one of this country's best known directors of Canadian work. With John van Burek he has translated seven plays of Michel Tremblay, and, on his own, Michel Marc Bouchard's *Les Grandes Chaleurs*.

ACT ONE

(1913. A fern and a small period chair. CORNELIA LAJEUNESSE is seated at the piano giving a lesson to a young pupil. She is well on in years and wears horn-rimmed glasses; energetic, a trifle eccentric, somewhat declamatory; given to gesticulating, as one would expect.)

(CORNELIA strikes a chord.)

EVA: *(Vocalizing.)* **A-a-a-a-a-**

CORNELIA: **As in an obstacle course, the voice must be able to clear the fence.** *(Striking a chord.)*

EVA: **A-a-a-a-a-**

CORNELIA: **No, no, that last note just tore its knickers.** *(Striking the chord again.)*

EVA: **A-a-a-a-a-**

CORNELIA: **Better!**

(Another chord. EVA sings again.)

Through the teeth, smile!

(The pupil produces an exaggerated smile, and the sound is clearer.)

(Chord, then vocalization.) **Lungs!**

(Chord, then vocalization.) **Don't expend it all, my child. Keep a little air in reserve, you don't want to play your last card too soon. I find you oddly distracted today. Concentrate, do you hear?**

EVA: **Yes, mademoiselle...or ought I to say madame?**

CORNELIA: *(Lifting her eyes from the piano; a beat.)* **Just mademoiselle, thank you.** *(She strikes a chord.)*

EVA: **A-a-a-a-a-a-a-**

CORNELIA: **No, no, no, not at all. What's wrong with you? Relax the shoulders, pull in the stomach. Imagine the note is a bird in your hand, you must hold it firmly without throttling it. Once again....** *(Chord.)*

EVA: **A-a-a-a-a-a-a-**

CORNELIA: **Much better. Another....** *(She strikes the chord. EVA makes no sound.)* **Now what's the matter?**

EVA: *(A beat.)* **Will I be able to see her today? Is she here?**

CORNELIA: **You're awfully curious.**

EVA: **Is Madame Albani here?**

CORNELIA: **Is that all you think about during your lessons? Seeing Albani?**

EVA: **I'm afraid so.**

CORNELIA: **You had trouble finding the three guineas to pay for a dozen lessons. Even if it's absurdly cheap, that's no reason to be daydreaming.**

EVA: **It's just that...I want so much to meet her. In Montreal she's all they talk about.**

              (A beat.)

CORNELIA: **Montreal.**

EVA: **I've read everything about her.**

CORNELIA: *(Amused.)* **Surely not. Come along now...smile, shoulders, stomach, and pull in the buttocks.** *(EVA obeys like a puppet. CORNELIA strikes a chord.)*

EVA: *(Complying.)* **A-a-a-a-a-**

CORNELIA: **Good. Rest.** *(She gets up.)* **Have you gone over the Irish ballad since last week?**

EVA: **Yes, Mademoiselle Cornelia.**

CORNELIA: We'll work on that after the next set of scales.

(EVA sighs. CORNELIA gives in.)

Yes, my sister is here.

EVA: Really? Do you think I could see her?

CORNELIA: I can't imagine what you're expecting.

EVA: I've dreamed of it so often, my unforgettable meeting with the great Albani, soprano of genius...

CORNELIA: Where did you pick that up? Albani is not a soprano of genius.

EVA: Everyone says so.

CORNELIA: And you? Have you heard her even once with your own ears? *(Testily.)* Albani is an artist who has had success, that's all. You must learn how to make distinctions. Don't go tossing around words like "great" and "genius". And bear in mind that talent has little to do with success.

(Calming down.)

Of course your point of view is perfectly valid. A workman's ear may think it is listening to a great soprano, whereas the *Times* critic hears only a screeching magpie. Or the reverse. It all depends on the ear. The songs, on the other hand, never change. And they last longer than the voice. Unfortunately in London workmens' ears are often dirty, hence people are inclined to accept the judgement of critics. What you have heard about my sister may in fact be worthless. I do not say that is the case, but you should allow for the possibility. The very first task for an artist anxious to succeed is to break with all received ideas. Never surrender to these opinions without first testing them yourself. For example...ferns. They say it's bad luck to have real plants on the stage. Ridiculous. Albani never gave a recital without her fern. So much for that superstition! *(As if confiding a great secret.)* The fern, you see, is as subtle as parsley. Always have a fern, it is the ideal companion to the music. Like parsley in some exquisite dish, the fern is elegant, and music is an elegant affair. *(A beat.)* Hmm?

EVA: I'm not sure that I understand your method, Mademoiselle Cornelia.

CORNELIA: My method.

EVA: Scales, scales, always scales...Before, my teachers would talk about the Italian school of singing, about German "soul" or the French style, but with you...I'm never sure what you want from me.

CORNELIA: I see...We're going to make conversation...so we won't have to do the scales.... *(She rises from the piano and with difficulty takes a few steps with her cane.)* **Just who do you think you are? Here you are in London, fresh off the boat, with a singing teacher chosen haphazardly from the Musical Directory, and you dare ask to which school this lady belongs?**

EVA: When I found out that you were...

CORNELIA: The sister of the great Albani, yes, I know. Listen to me carefully, child, it is 1913. It's no longer enough to wear pretty frocks and sing in tune. Properly speaking, there are only two methods of singing: the good and the bad. I teach the good.

Technique and soul. That is my method. Stop biting your lips like that, it's extremely annoying.

(A beat.)

The purpose of scales is to oil the machine, thereby permitting the soul to enter. When the machine is badly lubricated, the soul is simply *de trop*, like a grain of sand in the mechanism. Remember what I said to you last week...

EVA: A technician without soul is like an organ pipe.

CORNELIA: Precisely. One must strive for a balance between technique and soul. Effect a marriage of convenience between the two. Even in her greatest moments of triumph, my sister rigorously practised her scales. It is false to assume that scales are only for beginners.

They are a daily obligation.

EVA: *(Horrified.)* **Every day, till the end of my days?**

CORNELIA: *(Nodding in agreement.)* **You will scarcely make friends. It is not restful to have a neighbour who's forever practising her scales, there will be complaints. But if you practise your scales you will be solid, and solid, you will find success, and success will bring money, and money will permit you not to have neighbours, or at least to choose them better.**

Dimmi con chi vai e ti diro chi sei, as they say in Italy: tell me who your neighbours are, and I'll tell you about yourself. It's essential then to choose the right neighbours.

And to practise your scales.

(A beat.)

Take your place, now. From the beginning.

(She returns to the piano.)

If you don't stop biting your lips, they'll look like slippers the butler's dog has chewed.

EVA: **Why did Albani never go back to Canada?**

(A long beat.)

CORNELIA: **Here we go....** *(She plays several notes to alleviate her agitation.)*

Touch the throat. Breathe deeply. The voice is like the boat on which you've just come, resting on the waves of the ocean. Imagine the voice like a sailboat letting itself be rocked by the waves, by the scales.

(She strikes a chord.)

EVA: **A-a-a-a-a-**
A-a-a-a-a-

EMMA/EVA: **A-a-a-a-a-**
A-a-a-a-a-

(EMMA has entered. 1867. The deck of a ship sailing to England. EMMA and CORNELIA are seated on deck chairs, CORNELIA with a white silk scarf around her head.)

EMMA: A-a-a-a-a-
             E-e-e-e-e-
             I-i-i-i-i-

CORNELIA: Oh-oh-oh...Emma, I think I'm going to be sick. Stop, stop, I beg you. I'm not up to it.

EMMA: What do you think of Emma Bridgelake? *La Sonnambula* with Emma Bridgelake.... *(She laughs.)* I find that so amusing, don't you? Bridge-lake.... Papa would appreciate it.

CORNELIA: Especially after his fifth sherry.

EMMA: He would adore it.

CORNELIA: Emma, my stomach's in my throat.

EMMA: In three days it will all be over. We'll be landing in Southampton Friday. Do you need to lie down?

CORNELIA: No. Staying in bed is worse. Not to mention the racket next door.

EMMA: Poor woman, it's true, she was crying all night long. Must be someone who's left her country for good. Do you suppose she's left her family behind?

CORNELIA: Emma, you are so naïve. That woman was not crying, not at all...if you get my drift.

EMMA: Of course she was crying. She kept on moaning, as if she were calling out to someone.... Massimo, she was saying, Massimo...as if she were calling a child left behind on the shore.

CORNELIA: No doubt. And the bearded man who shares her cabin was standing by with his handkerchief. What time is it?

EMMA: He's an Italian, you know. A real Italian. Four o'clock. And so polite. My goodness, they're well-bred, those Italians. Yesterday I asked his permission to practise my scales out here on the deck, and in the most beautiful accent he replied, "Signorina, it is I who must ask permission to listen." He even knew some of the arias. He told me it had been the dream of his life to sing opera, like all Italians. But since a career is so taxing, he didn't have the stamina for it.

CORNELIA: You must have enjoyed hearing that.

EMMA: He could have been a tenor. She, she doesn't sing at all, of course, but she's very pleasant.

CORNELIA: In that case, if the occasion presents itself, ask them to sing 'The child left behind on the shore' *sotto voce* tonight. It will help me sleep. God, my stomach!

EMMA: Look out there, it's much calmer…. What do you see?

CORNELIA: Water, nothing but water….

EMMA: Away out there is the Irish Sea.

CORNELIA: If you can see that, your eyesight's amazing.

EMMA: It'll be supper time soon. You'll feel less grumpy after you've eaten.

CORNELIA: Eaten what? That nondescript mush that tastes like chalk? I tell you, Emma, if it were just me, I'd be on the next ship home.

EMMA: It's the price one pays, Cornelia. Remember what Papa said. To become a great artist, one must be prepared to pay the price.

CORNELIA: If that's the case, why isn't he here to pay it with us?

EMMA: Feel the wind. Breathe.

CORNELIA: I've been feeling the wind for eight days.

EMMA: You don't appreciate our good fortune. How many girls our age are lucky enough to cross the Atlantic? Just think, I'm going in quest of all those legendary characters, all those fabulous roles that await me.

CORNELIA: There's nothing lucky about crossing the Atlantic, it's torture. As for your "quest," you're going to look for a singing teacher, and all that's "awaiting" us at Southampton is that nun the Mother Superior wrote to.

EMMA: If I'd known you were going to be so disagreeable, I'd never have insisted you come.

CORNELIA: You didn't have to insist, Emma, Papa did it for you. He wasn't about to let his nightingale of Albany leave home without her sister to "accompany" her. Especially when it's thanks to her no one notices when you start adding notes, or "embellishing," as you call it.

EMMA: Embellishing? Me?

CORNELIA: Yes, Emma, endlessly.

EMMA: Well, even so, they'd hardly know the difference…those Philistines we're leaving in our wake…That's all about to change, finally we're going somewhere where people *know*…

CORNELIA: Honestly! Those Philistines organized concerts and I don't know how many receptions to make it possible for you to make this trip!

EMMA: *(Absorbed.)* Do you remember? The girls of Chambly who used to sneer at us when we couldn't come out to play? Today they must be biting their lips in envy.

CORNELIA: The girls of Chambly are assembling their trousseaux. And if they're biting anything, it's not their lips, but their suitors'. For some people, singing lullabyes to their children is happiness enough.

EMMA: You understand nothing. You don't see, Destiny picks out a path for each of us, you've only to follow it…. How do you know that Destiny hasn't picked out a wonderful suitor for you in the streets of London or the parks of Paris?

CORNELIA: You must be joking.

EMMA: You don't believe in Destiny? Four years ago who would have suspected that I would sing in front of the King of England?

CORNELIA: Not the King of England, Emma, the Prince of Wales.

EMMA: It's the same thing...they'll end up crowning him. Any day now, his mother's going to die of grief. I wouldn't give her a year.

CORNELIA: You talk as if you knew her.

EMMA: I have every intention of meeting her. If it's meant to be. Destiny...like at Mechanic's Hall: one only had to be there at the right moment. Papa could have had us sing elsewhere, the Prince might have cancelled, I could have sung badly...

CORNELIA: You did...and to cover your tracks, I played louder. *(They laugh.)*

EMMA: A mere quarter tone. But you'll see, or rather, you'll hear, a difference one year from now.

CORNELIA: How? Does your Destiny include a singing teacher who can work miracles?

EMMA: Precisely.

CORNELIA: Who'll give us a place to sleep, the wherewithal to buy costumes for the great roles, decent clothes to wear when your bosom friend, Queen Victoria, invites us to tea?

EMMA: Why not?

CORNELIA: You're mad.

EMMA: You must believe in it, Cornelia. Without it, none of this makes sense.

CORNELIA: So it's important what I think? That's new. Well, time will tell. If nothing else happens, at least we'll see some countries.

EMMA: England first, then...then Paris. Singing lessons, six months, a provincial opera house or two, and then.... "A young woman who sings more sweetly than the birds." You read the papers, don't you?

CORNELIA: Be quiet, Emma, your modesty's making the boat rock.

(A beat.)

EMMA: You must excuse me, I have to work.

CORNELIA: Work, work, always work…

               (Another beat. EMMA is vocalizing.)

CORNELIA: And love? *(EMMA pretends not to hear.)* Emma!

EMMA: Yes?

CORNELIA: At our age, girls talk about love. We never do. Why is that?

EMMA: Do I know?

CORNELIA: Perhaps you should have been a nun after all. Men hardly seem to interest you.

EMMA: Boys are so vulgar…their preoccupations so …terrestrial.

CORNELIA: What I wouldn't give right now for a terrestrial occupation….

EMMA: They're always wanting to get close to you, touch you…as soon as no one's looking.

CORNELIA: What are you talking about? You've never even been alone with a man.

EMMA: How would you know?

CORNELIA: Their names.

EMMA: Well…there's Papa…

CORNELIA: Papa doesn't count, he's not a man, he's a father. Men…they're so intriguing, and a bit frightening. I love that dark beard of the captain's…it's so mysterious.

               (CORNELIA laughs.)

EMMA: What?

CORNELIA: Did you know that when I'd inquire about boys at the convent they'd always say to me, "Ask your big sister."

My big sister was always at the piano, or practising her scales, or listening to her father describe the balls she'd someday attend if she never stopped slaving. God, how I hated that dark wood in the piano room. Love...I found it wherever I could...in your arms, Emma, on stormy nights...

EMMA: Cornelia!

CORNELIA: We could have been at home at this hour...smelling soup, not salt...

EMMA: It's always difficult at first, you'll get used to it. When we left Chambly for Albany, you couldn't stop crying; afterwards you never wanted to leave...It will be the same over there.

CORNELIA: I'm nineteen, Emma. I'm seasick. They were always entertaining, our games, our dreams. But this, this is life, Emma, real life. On a boat headed towards a country we don't know, full of people we don't know...

EMMA: Cornelia, you're boring.

(Silence. A bit of wind perhaps. EMMA softly sings to herself "She is Far From the Land.")

CORNELIA: *(To her pupil.)* **Softly, but not too. The lady is leaving her native land, and as the shore fades from view she tries to fasten on memories of landscapes and people she has loved. The song is sad, but it's the public that must cry, not the singer.**

(EVA sings, "She is Far From the Land." After the song, with a wave of her hand, EMMA acknowledges with enthusiasm the applause of her fellow passengers.)

EMMA: That's an Irish song I've just learned. A lady from Boston in First Class taught it to me. The man at our table told me I have good teeth, and that that's very important for a singer. Did you know that a gap in the teeth is a sign of generosity?

CORNELIA: I thought that the sign of generosity was to give.

EMMA: What's wrong with you, Cornelia? Ten days ago you

couldn't wait to see Europe, and now...pcht! Have you lost your taste for adventure? Remember when we said good-bye to Papa in New York, you could barely contain your excitement.

CORNELIA: I don't feel we're in the same boat now.... Ten days ago, it's true, we were leaving together. Cornelia and Emma were leaving for Europe.... Now I feel like one of your suitcases.

EMMA: Here we go again.

CORNELIA: Really, if you could see yourself...We've become so *grande dame*...curtsies here, curtsies there, a witty word to Madame, a compliment to Monsieur.... Do you realize you're speaking to perfect strangers? At the table you toss off remarks to all and sundry, you force yourself into conversations...and you've introduced me to no one. It's as if I don't exist...

EMMA: It's not my fault if you never say a word....

CORNELIA: There's no need, you answer for me...It's as if you were ashamed...Yesterday at supper, if you could have heard yourself: "Truly, I do not understand how or what it is, but I feel there is something in me which I must do, which will be my duty to do." Like some penny dreadful! You were perfectly ridiculous.

EMMA: Ridiculous?

CORNELIA: "I never had a doll!" And in your best British accent. "I never had a doll!"

EMMA: But it's true! I never had dolls, I spent my days in the music room, at the piano.

CORNELIA: Of course you spent your days at the piano, but think back...You had dolls, dozens of them: wooden dolls, woolen dolls, even porcelain. The truth, Emma, is that you hated dolls. Dolls to you are insignificant, worthless. And so you say, "I never had a doll," and everyone says "poor little thing."

             For you it's only the piano and singing that count...the work is like a sickness, you're incapable of being amused. Papa's delusions of grandeur have made you so ambitious, it's embarrassing. But that you won't say at the captain's table, just as you can't admit that the couple in the next cabin are making love, and that when she "cries," as you say, it's from pleasure...

EMMA: I'm going to be ill.... Oh my God, I'm going to be ill! *(She gets up and runs out.)*

CORNELIA: Emma! I'm the one who's seasick! *(She looks around and realizes she's made a fool of herself. She pulls herself together and sits down again. To her pupil.)* **That's fine, but the legato's missing. I played you a calm sea, you have sung me a choppy one. The accompaniment is not a walking stick, mademoiselle, it is the walk itself. Stop biting your lips like that, it's unbearable.**

(1871. The offices of Covent Garden, London. A waiting room, Turkish carpet, a chair, a piano. EMMA enters in a state of excitement impossible to hide. She places everything in CORNELIA's arms: parcels, accessories, scores.)

EMMA: I don't see why you're so upset.

CORNELIA: They drag us from one antechamber to the next. Everyone gives us these superior little glances, ever so English. If they took us seriously they wouldn't make us wait.

EMMA: We've been waiting two months, another ten minutes won't kill us.

CORNELIA: I've got mud all over my hem. It's so filthy here, I've never seen so many people in the streets. And they're always lining up!

EMMA: We won't be in line for long. I've prepared quite a surprise for Mr Mapleson. The only thing is, his secretary seemed a bit surprised to see us. He smiled at you, didn't he? He must like your accent.

CORNELIA: You did all the talking, I didn't say a word. But he's a good-looking boy. He'll do.

EMMA: That's all you ever think about.

CORNELIA:	*(Laughing.)* Yes.
EMMA:	My hands are like ice.
CORNELIA:	Stop worrying.
EMMA:	It's as if they weren't expecting us.... You're right, they don't take us seriously.... "Soooo...you're from the colonies?" I must be quiet, save my voice.
CORNELIA:	Exactly.
EMMA:	The scores, you have them?
CORNELIA:	Yes.
EMMA:	Good. I won't say another word. *(Pause.)* You, you may speak if you wish.
CORNELIA:	Thank you.
EMMA:	Do you think it'll take place here?
CORNELIA:	Save your voice.
EMMA:	Yes. But do you...
CORNELIA:	Emma!
EMMA:	Yes, yes, I'll be quiet.
CORNELIA:	It must be here, there's a piano.
EMMA:	There's a piano. *(As if the idea suddenly strikes her.)* Of course.... Find the Bellini and go to the piano.
CORNELIA:	We can't just do that!
EMMA:	Of course we can. We're doing it.
CORNELIA:	*(To EVA.)* **The accompaniment is an art in itself, mademoiselle; be always considerate of your accompanist. It is a humble position, but without it the music is naked. You accompanist is your accomplice, not a negligable quantity. Especially during the bows. Do you see, mademoiselle, I chose to be an accompanist, nobody twisted my arm. Do you follow me?**

Today we shall work on "Ah non giunge!" A song of joy taken from *La Sonnambula* **of Bellini, a cock-and-bull, but utterly charming, story of a young girl who falls asleep in everybody's bed and can't understand why her fiancé takes offence. In the second act, when everyone in this Swiss village finally sees the light and realizes that Amina is suffering from an acute case of naïvete, Amina launches hysterically into an expression of the most profound joy by singing....** *(To EMMA.)* With or without the recitative?

EMMA: Without.

CORNELIA: *Ah, non credea mirarti, si presto estinto, o fiore....* **Oh, flowers, I would not have believed you could fade so soon.... Off we go...and pay attention to your gestures....**

> *(EVA sings "Ah! non credea mirarti" from Bellini's "La Sonnambula.")*

Not bad, but I'm not sure you understand what she's saying.

EVA: **Neither does the audience.**

CORNELIA: Maybe so, but you don't gesture enough.

EMMA: She's crying from joy, Cornelia, the house is not on fire.

CORNELIA: Eivino is on his knees, he's just given her back her *ring*, her ring, do you understand, her ring.... He's on his knees telling her he's going to marry her...

EMMA: No question, if you could have a man on his knees you'd dance the quadrille with both arms in the air.

CORNELIA: You're not listening to me, I'm doing this to help you....

EMMA: If you really want to help, play a bit faster, it's like a funeral march....

> *(They are interrupted by the arrival of FREDERIC GYE.)*

FREDERIC: *(Going spontaneously to CORNELIA.)* Mademoiselle Lajeunesse! It's you.... What a remarkable timbre…even from a distance—I was in the other room, I dared not enter for fear of interrupting such a marvel— an effortless delivery, and without exaggeration… *(Turning to EMMA.)* And you must be the accompanist? A remarkable tempo.

EMMA: No, Mr Mapleson, I am Emma Lajeunesse…. It is me that you heard.

FREDERIC: Oh! Really? Then you are….

CORNELIA: I am Cornel…

EMMA: My sister Cornelia Lajeunesse, my accompanist.

CORNELIA: That's right.

FREDERIC: How very amusing…how very amusing. What a charming little blunder…. Mademoiselle Lajeunesse, I was aware that you were coming, but I wasn't expecting you today.

EMMA: But I had a letter sent this week.

FREDERIC: A misunderstanding there as well, perhaps? And to be perfectly frank, I doubt I should have allowed you to sing for me….

EMMA: *(Hastily.)* Mr Mapleson, I realize you are an extremely busy man, and I have perhaps abused your patience in having the audacity to sing without even waiting to be asked, but the piano was there, inviting, smiling, with all its keys, so that I really could not resist the temptation…

           (CORNELIA rolls her eyes in exasperation.)

FREDERIC: But you have done very well…otherwise I should have missed hearing a very remarkable artist.

EMMA: Mr Mapleson.

FREDERIC: I assure you. I know myself, I might have shown you the door on the pretext of having too many sopranos in my service.

EMMA: I have brought with me some letters of recommendation…. Cornelia!

(CORNELIA goes to the satchel.)

FREDERIC: That will not be necessary, Mademoiselle Lajeunesse, or, perhaps I might call you Emma?

EMMA: I should be honoured, Mr Mapleson.

FREDERIC: And you, Cornelia? Like old Lear's daughter, how very amusing.

CORNELIA: In Shakespeare's play it's Cordelia.

EMMA: Cornelia!

CORNELIA: I beg your pardon.

FREDERIC: But no, you're right. Cordelia. We English are such dreadful chauvinists, we think we know our authors backwards. But, as the unfortunate Desdemona says, "What's in a name?" A name is never just a name.

EMMA: *(Laughing to excuse CORNELIA.)* How right you are, Mr Mapleson.

FREDERIC: But Lajeunesse will never do. Too long, too French. We must find something with an Italian ring to it. But first things first. What's next, then? Papers.... Contract! Obviously the season is too advanced for you to be a part of it, and all my singers have understudies waiting for one of them to miss her footing on the staircase.

I shall make you a proposition, we'll discuss it, and if it suits you, we'll be in business.

Well, well, well. Let's have a look a next season's calendar.

CORNELIA: Emma knows the whole of Bellini by heart. Papa taught her everything.

FREDERIC: Bellini was a friend of mine.

CORNELIA: She can go on at twenty-four hours' notice with her eyes closed.

EMMA: Cornelia, please. Not in front of Mr Mapleson.

FREDERIC: Mademoiselle Cornelia, it is not my custom to negotiate in the presence of family members, hence I would ask that you kindly wait for us in the adjoining room. My son will keep you company.

CORNELIA: But....

EMMA: Go, Cornelia.

CORNELIA: Very well. You mean, the gentleman out front?

FREDERIC: Ernest. He will look after you. I believe there's some tea left.

EVA: **That was a daring thing to do!**

CORNELIA: **If you like. But look what happened....**

                (She goes.)

EMMA: You must excuse my sister, she doesn't really know the customs.... In fact, she's a bit...well, you see, she insisted on accompanying me.

FREDERIC: A thing she does splendidly. An excellent touch. Yes, yes, well....

                Emma, I shan't keep secrets from you.... At this moment I am tasting the joys of a truce with one of my protégées, a very great artist, though a veritable shrew. If I take you with me today, there will either be peace or a resumption of hostilities. I am, however, prepared to run that risk.

EMMA: Is it a firm offer?

FREDERIC: You have costumes?

EMMA: I have all of Amina's gowns.

FREDERIC: New ones?

EMMA: The Messina production.

FREDERIC: You might as well have nothing. The London public are not keen on second hand. And languages?

EMMA: I have a good English and my Italian is improving, I work at it every day. French, obviously.

FREDERIC: Obviously, yes, obviously. No German?

EMMA: Not so much.

FREDERIC: Hmm....

EMMA: But still, a little. I'm working on it as well.

FREDERIC: You must. Soon everything will be sung in German. The opera of the future, breaking new ground.

EMMA: If necessary, I'll take private lessons. Mr Mapleson, I assure you, you will never have occasion to complain of me.

FREDERIC: I should like so much to be able to promise you the same. I am demanding, Mademoiselle Lajeunesse—no, no, no, Lajeunesse will never do—demanding and merciless. I expect from my artists a staunch loyalty.

EMMA: I shall do exactly as you tell me.

FRDERIC: Not so fast, my dear.... You will see, more enticing offers will come your way and the temptation to forget your obligations to an old goat like me will be considerable. I give advice, and good advice it is, but the proof of it is not always plain to see. Do I make myself clear? Pray, what do you know of me?

EMMA: Mr Mapleson, I know that you are the most important, nay, the most eminent director of opera in Europe. It is not for nothing I have undertaken such a lengthy journey just to meet you.

FREDERIC: And my rivals? You have heard about them?

EMMA: We speak only of you in foreign parts, Mr Mapleson. All the others rest, so to speak, in the giant's shade.

FREDERIC: Hmm-hm.

EMMA: I could have introduced myself elsewhere, but I chose to measure myself against the best.

FREDERIC: Well, well, well. So much is clear. I'm impressed you know with whom you are dealing. I'm going to have you sign an agreement in principle which will guarantee me exclusivity. Of course, you can make use of your summer, however it suits you, to review with the help of your singing coach the role of Amina.

EMMA: You mean it? I will make my debut with *La Sonnambula*?

FREDERIC: I shall have to confer with my directors, but I think it will fit comfortably into our next season. Of course, you have just made an enemy, I promised the revival to Adelina Patti.

EMMA: La Patti! It's like a dream. All these names, suddenly a part of my life, Mapleson, La Patti, London!

FREDERIC: And here is my first piece of advice: avoid London.

EMMA: You mean, stay away?

FREDERIC: I warned you my advice would not always be self-evident. Do not be seen in society, steer clear of the priviledged milieu, let the name of Emma hover tantalizingly in the air. You must never be seen here...and especially not heard. Having to wait, you see, will make them so greedy, so thirsty to hear you, that we shall find ourselves the toast of next season. You were born in...

EMMA: Montreal. Chambly, to be precise...

FREDERIC: Chambly. Yes, yes, yes. And where is that?

EMMA: In Lower Canada.

FREDERIC: Of course. *(A beat.)* Yes, that will be fine. Canada. I have never been there. It is very...very picturesque, is it not?

EMMA: Oh, yes. *(A beat.)* Mr Mapleson, my sister and I have very little at our disposal...

FREDERIC: An advance? By all means. Well, I'll get everything ready. This is merely an agreement in principle. You sign here. Dear Emma, I believe Heaven has sent you to us.

(CORNELIA bursts into the room.)

CORNELIA: Don't sign!

EMMA: Cornelia!

CORNELIA: *(Seeing FREDERIC take hold of the document.)* You've signed?

EMMA: Cornelia, for Heaven's sake!

EVA: *(Laughing.)* **You were not in the right place.**

CORNELIA: *(To EVA.)* **It was his son who told me that.** *(To EMMA.)* We are not at the Royal Italian Opera and this man is not Mapleson!

EMMA: What is this nonsense? You're perfectly ridiculous. Mr Mapleson, pray excuse my sister.

CORNELIA: Covent Garden. The coachman misunderstood us. We're in the wrong place.

(A beat. They look at each other for a long moment.)

FREDERIC: Frederic Gye is my name. I am the Manager of Covent Garden. Mr Mapleson is at Her Majesty's a few streets away. A few streets, that's hardly anything, but in London it can make all the difference.

(EMMA is dumbfounded, then smiles at her stupidity.)

EMMA: May I sit down?

FREDERIC: Yes, well, in effect it's a charming little blunder. I am prepared, if you like, to tear up this paper and forget that I ever saw you. Though I could never forget having heard you, even if I wished it. I doubt that Mapleson will grant you an audition if he learns that you found your way here first. I am prepared to say nothing of this incident and to leave you at liberty to pursue your ambition of placing yourself under the protection of…the giant's wing. However, I believe in destiny. You would never have come here otherwise. You *are* La Sonnambula, Emma. You walk in your sleep, and just like her you end up in the wrong bed sometimes. Covent Garden is the right bed for you. Do you agree?

EMMA: *(She looks to CORNELIA for approval.)* I believe that I do.

FREDERIC: They will come, they will listen, and they will come again. You know , Mademoiselle Lajeunesse, in England we never forget. *(He goes to leave.)* Oh, and work on your German.

CORNELIA: *(To EVA.)* **A knowledge of tongues, not all of them, but the civilized ones, is essential. It is all very well for a singer to know how to pronounce the words, but to understand the sense of each, that is her trump card. Do you follow me?**

EVA: **Yes, Mademoiselle.**

CORNELIA: **The *sostenuto*, which is pertinent to this aria, is the art of sustaining a note or a series of notes in a constant legato. Not to be confused with the drawing out of a note that certain sopranos are inclined to favour. Who think of it as their "signature."**

              (She plays a little.)

              "The note is pretty, I produce it gracefully, therefore I shall prolong it." Ridiculous. The temptation to hold on to a note in this meaningless way occurs frequently at the end of an aria. It is pure indulgence. Like a second helping of dessert. It behooves any artist to have a *sostenuto* as remarkable on the stage as in real life.

              (EMMA enters running, interrupting the lesson. She is twenty-five years old.)

EMMA: Cornelia, listen to this! *The Musical Times*, May, 1872: "The great event of the month has been the success of Mademoiselle Albani, who has made her debut as Amina in *La Sonnambula*. With a genuine soprano voice, a facile and unexaggerated execution, and a remarkable power of *sostenuto* in the higher part of her register, this young vocalist at once secured the good opinion of her audience. Except for her physical person, which, although agreeable enough, fails to correspond to the ravishing portraits of the diva we have seen in the windows of the editor Girod...." Honestly....

CORNELIA: I told you that portrait doesn't look like you.

EMMA: "…of the editor Girod, Mlle Albani lived up to all our expectations." They call me the daughter of Bellini. Do you realize that this little article is going to change our lives? Words in a column. Just words printed in a newspaper.

(She goes out.)

EVA: **Mademoiselle…**

CORNELIA: **Yes?**

EVA: **I don't understand, a *sostenuto* as remarkable on the stage as in real life…**

CORNELIA: **Ah yes, by that I mean that, as in her art, a soprano must in her life hold on to a series of small personal victories, and not stretch out a triumph indefinitely. You understand me, don't you?**

(We hear the opening measures of the aria, "Qui la voce," from Bellini's "I Puritani." The great doors open and Elvira—played by EMMA—enters, a wedding veil in her hands. The lighting must come from the footlights. It is the scene in the castle. EMMA's make-up must be exaggerated, with strong shadings in the Victorian manner, and a very long wig of dark, straight hair. She opens her mouth to begin the aria, but it is the pupil who sings while the lights are lowered on EMMA. At the conclusion of the aria, however, it is EMMA, and not EVA, who takes the bows.)

(Aria: "Qui la voce." Once the aria is finished, EMMA makes her lengthy bows in an affected manner. She then sweeps out the doors which close behind her. We are now in a dressing room in Covent Garden in 1874 between the second and third acts of Bellini's "I Puritani.")

EMMA: *(Entering, out of breath.)* Unbelievable! Shall I tell you something amazing?

CORNELIA: *(Without enthusiasm.)* By all means…. *(She steps behind EMMA and starts to dress her wig.)*

EMMA: I could have sung it twice if I'd wanted to. *(CORNELIA has mimed EMMA's words.)*

CORNELIA: Really?

EMMA: I had them like *that* in the palm of my hand. *(Again CORNELIA mimes her words.)*

CORNELIA: You don't say…

EMMA: I wonder if she was sleeping.

CORNELIA: Ernest told me earlier that she smiled after the first act. It's a good sign. Though that might just be because Charles the First's widow managed to escape. Ernest was so funny; he said, "Wait till she finds out what happens in the end."

EMMA: *(Stung.)* She knows very well how it ends. They're her ancestors, after all. Careful, that hurts…you're pulling my hair!

CORNELIA: That would surprise me, Emma.

EMMA: And why is that?

CORNELIA: It's a wig.

EMMA: Oh, leave it alone!

CORNELIA: *Mille pardons, majesté.*

EMMA: Hand me the brush, I'll do it myself.

CORNELIA: Performing for royalty doesn't agree with you?

EMMA: Did you spend the entire second act chatting with Ernest?

CORNELIA: Except for your *aires, majesté*…. I wouldn't have missed them for all the tea in China. *(A beat.)* You were very good.

EMMA: I was excellent. Are you in love with him?

CORNELIA: What?

EMMA: You heard me. Are you in love with the manager's son?

CORNELIA: Why do you say that?

EMMA: Why not? It's all you talk about.... Are you in love?

CORNELIA: It's like a sickness. Are you in love? Have you got a cold? Do you feel queasy? Are you in love?

EMMA: Of course you are, just as I thought. Doting fool! If you think I'm about to sacrifice Heaven knows what for your shenanigans....

CORNELIA: I've nothing to sacrifice, Emma. You're the diva. I'm not obliged to submit to the ten commandments of Frederic Gye, thank you very much.

EMMA: Which are?

CORNELIA: Not to speak, to receive no one, to liven up one's poor tired voice for at least an hour each day, eat little, drink only warm milk, abstain from all rich foods that might affect one's breathing or make the stomach swell, avoid all physical exercise, long walks, any reading that tires the mind; but especially, especially never laugh out loud, and never cry. All that, just to be able to sing in the evening. Would you mind telling me what's left?

EMMA: I won't answer that. I have to save my voice.

CORNELIA: Not everyone thinks like you that opera is the be-all and end-all. Ernest thinks...

EMMA: Again!

CORNELIA: Ernest believes that life is more important than the theatre.

EMMA: That's easy for someone whose father has seen to everything to assure him a comfortable future.

CORNELIA: We too, Emma, we had a father who saw to everything.

EMMA: How can you compare them?

CORNELIA: Papa saw to everything. His eyes weren't as good as Frederic Gye's, that's all.

EMMA: How can you expect the public to appreciate the courage, the self-denial it takes to stir their emotions and ravish their senses when your own sister makes light of everything?

CORNELIA: Who are you talking to, the walls? I wasn't making light of anything. I simply said it wasn't the be-all and end-all.

EMMA: How pedestrian!

CORNELIA: Emma, even the Queen of England goes to sleep at concerts.

EMMA: *(Dressing her hair at the mirror and touching up her make-up.)* She fell asleep?

CORNELIA: For a little.

EMMA: That's because she has a great many responsibilities, she doesn't spend her days chasing husbands, she...

> *(During the last five speeches QUEEN VICTORIA has entered.)*

CORNELIA: *(Seeing her.)* Oh, *Majesté! (She curtsies.)*

EMMA: Stop your nonsense and pass me a pin! I don't know what's up with the tenor this evening, his "personal secretary" must not have come home last night.... Pass me a pin.... *(The QUEEN moves toward the table, takes a pin and hands her one.)* Thank you. *(EMMA continues to make-up.)*

CORNELIA: Emma.

EMMA: What is it?

CORNELIA: Someone's here.

EMMA: *(Preoccupied.)* Is that my dress for Act III? *(She gives a rapid glance.)* That's right, love, put it on the chair.... *(She looks again.)* Oh, my God, Your Majesty! *(She prostrates herself.)* A thousand pardons, I had no idea that it....

VICTORIA: We are sorry to surprise you like this, but our happiness was so complete, we wanted to express our gratitude without delay.

EMMA: Your Majesty, the honour is too great.

VICTORIA: You have awakened us from a long sleep, Mademoiselle Albani.

EMMA: I'm so ashamed, I never wished to displease Your Majesty.

VICTORIA: That would hardly be possible. Please, rise. *(To CORNELIA.)* You, as well. Too many people close to the ground gives us vertigo. You have awakened us from a long sleep, it is our first visit to the opera since the death of our beloved consort. A treat we have deprived ourselves of for far too long. *(She smiles.)* We had forgotten all this beauty.... Did you know there was a time when we dedicated ourselves to the pleasures of music? Oh, yes! Our dear husband delighted in playing the piano. He liked to assure us that we could more or less sing in tune. Such a marvellous humour. But after hearing you, our lyric experiments seem like child's play. We are always so amazed by the memory, how do you manage to retain all those notes? We still have to be prompted for the words to "God Save the Queen." How warm it is!

EMMA: Would Your Majesty care to sit down?

VICTORIA: You are too kind.

EMMA: Cornelia, be so good as to fetch a chair. *(She does so.)*

VICTORIA: Listening to you, my dear, the Queen was often on the verge of tears. You are a veritable magician, Mademoiselle Albani, and we have literally fallen beneath your spell.

> *(She looks at CORNELIA as one might regard a small animal.)*

VICTORIA: And you are?

> *(CORNELIA is dumbfounded.)*

EMMA: Your Majesty, Cornelia is my sister.

VICTORIA: Really! Are you a musician as well? *(Again CORNELIA is taken aback.)* I take it you have a tongue. Was it not you who was commenting a moment ago on the Queen's listening habits?

EMMA: Cornelia accompanies me on the piano, she oversees my rehearsals.

VICTORIA: How very convenient. Now, my child, leave us, if you will. We should like to have a conversation with our *grande artiste*.

CORNELIA: *(Visibly moved by the QUEEN's presence.) Majesté. (She goes out.)*

　　　　　　(VICTORIA sits down and drops the royal "We's.")

VICTORIA: It's the most uncomfortable throne I've occupied for a very long time. But the real queen of the evening is you, Mademoiselle Albani. By the way, why Albani? We were wondering about that at Windsor this morning.

EMMA: Your Majesty, my father was an organist at Albany in the state of New York when I was a child, and I fancied it might be a good omen.

VICTORIA: I gathered you were a Canadian subject.

EMMA: I am, Your Majesty.

VICTORIA: You sang for my son, the Prince of Wales, several years ago in Montreal; he refers to it still as a rapturous occasion. My son is a great lover of opera. A very great lover, I'm afraid. He goes incessantly. Even during the week. In Paris he is not called *le Prince de Galles*, but *le prince gaulois*. That's because he has a gift for enjoyment, or *le sens de la fête*, as they say in France. Do your people say that as well?

EMMA: Yes, Your Majesty, I believe so.

VICTORIA: *(Very interested.)* Mademoiselle Albani, tell me, do you have *le sens de la fête*?

EMMA: I couldn't say, Your Majesty.

VICTORIA: If it's clear to you that you have *le sens de la fête*, you must explain to me how it works. I think about it often, but understanding seems to elude me. Celebrations bore me royally, as a rule. No pun intended. *(A beat.)* I imagined you much smaller. *(With interest.)* And you, how did you imagine me? Am I different? *(She laughs. EMMA does not reply.)* Aren't you afraid when you're standing at the top of that enormous staircase? I was dreadfully afraid for you. Once on a state visit I missed a step and nobody laughed except me. I find it so amusing when someone misses a step.

I am very partial to Verdi, the poor man must have suffered terribly. I realize that taste is a personal matter, but your colleague who's singing Lord Walton is far too stout for the role. There's something wonderfully fishy about a leader of the Puritans who's fat. *(She gets up and moves around the dressing room.)* They look after you well here?

EMMA: Oh, very well, Your Majesty. Mr Gye is very considerate of his artists.

VICTORIA: Does Mr Gye have *le sens de la fête*? There's such an atmosphere reigns in the theatre. One hears so much about people in the musical world. They say you're always surrounded by friends, a *coterie*, I believe it's called, and that you laugh a lot. *(A beat.)* Do you laugh a lot? There's so little occasion to these days. I'm at the age when one loses all one's friends. I should like you to sing for me at Windsor...a private concert. Perhaps you would include your *"Qui la voce?"* I am so fond of Verdi.

EMMA: Bellini, Your Majesty.

VICTORIA: What did you say?

EMMA: The opera...

VICTORIA: Yes.

EMMA: The opera is...is by Bellini.

VICTORIA: Good Heavens, how dreadful! We are not amused.

EMMA: Forgive me, Your Majesty....

VICTORIA: No, no, it is me you must forgive.... *(She laughs.)* We shall be friends, you and I. Truly, you're one of the few that has ever tried to correct me. They'd sooner change the name in the programme than tell me I was wrong. I terrify them. *(She laughs again.)* Really, had I said that in front of others, *I Puritani* would have become an opera by Verdi. And here was I about to congratulate Maestro Tosti. You have saved me from a very uncomfortable situation. Italians are so easily offended. *(She has walked*

all around the room, and now stops in front of the chair.)
You must ask Mr Gye to find you a more suitable
armchair. You will come to Windsor next month and we
will talk about music. Are you familiar with Gounod?

EMMA: Yes, Your Majesty, Gounod has written some lovely
                things.

VICTORIA: *Faust,* heavenly *Faust!* When your colleague Madame
                Patti came to Windsor, she sang the *Jewel Song* for us.

EMMA: If it would please Her Majesty, I could sing for her some
                airs from the opera I am presently rehearsing.

VICTORIA: How is that? You mean to say that I'd hear them before
                anyone else? How very exciting, I'm awfully tempted.
                (Confidentially.) Of what opera do we speak?

EMMA: *Lohengrin,* Your Majesty, by Wagner.

VICTORIA: Oh, Wagner! Wagner? Germany and her drums! Utterly
                incomprehensible, Mademoiselle Albani. The most
                harebrained plots, no melodies, and nothing to take home
                with you. Sometimes at the palace I discover my ladies-
                in-waiting humming some Verdi, even Rossini. But no
                one could possibly hum Wagner!

EMMA: Wagner is the music of the future, Your Majesty.

VICTORIA: *(Flaring up.)* The future bores me, Mademoiselle
                Albani, and I don't wish to hear of it. The past has the
                advantage of being an inexhaustible source of
                conversations. And conversation is the prerogative of
                civilized peoples. The future! The future provokes only
                debate, and I have a horror of debates. I leave all that to
                Mr Gladstone and his Liberals! Understand me, I
                shouldn't want you to think that I'm…"old hat," isn't
                that the phrase? On the contrary, Handel I find tiring, and
                I shan't pretend that I like him. *(She notices the effect her
                words have had on EMMA.)* I have frightened you. I did
                not mean to. *(She approaches EMMA and touches her
                cheek.)* The Queen is going to leave you now. You must
                prepare. *(Confidingly.)* I am so eager to know the ending.
                I hope it is a happy one…like Faust. When Marguerite
                calls out to the angels who are to save her… *(She sings,
                rather badly:)* "Anges purs, anges radieux." The voices

rise, Marguerite's rises higher, and suddenly she dies. *(Somber voice.)* "*Jugé*," exults Mephistopheles. The music continues…"Sauvée," the angels reply! *(She sighs with happiness.)* Oh…. Heavenly! Such a pleasure it has been to meet you. I'm longing to talk music with you again. You must include some Gounod. You are on the threshold of a long and exciting career, Mademoiselle Albani. I shall personally see to it that my little Canadian will always have the warmest of welcomes.

EMMA: I thank Your Majesty, but I am unworthy of such an honour.

VICTORIA: You are worthy of all that's happened to you, never doubt it. You are the wood from which great flutes are made. *(She goes to leave, stops at the door and turns.)* The music of the future, you say? Include an aria of Herr Wagner in the programme of your recital. Hearing it sung by you, who knows, perhaps the Queen may learn something.

> *(She goes out. We hear the start of the third act of I Puritani. EMMA remains alone on the stage for a moment, somewhat troubled. She touches her cheek where the QUEEN touched it and is suddenly filled with an overwhelming sense of power. She smiles openly. CORNELIA returns.)*

CORNELIA: What did she say to you?

EMMA: Can you imagine? The Queen of England! The Empress of India! Oh, Cornelia, it really happened! *(Filled with an immense joy, EMMA throws her arms around CORNELIA and embraces her wildly.)* Didn't I tell you so? Thank you, Cornelia, thank you for having faith in our dreams. Can you feel it—her presence is everywhere, it hovers in the room.

CORNELIA: What hovers?

EMMA: The force, the power. Ah…she is a real person, not just an image. The Widow of Windsor was really here.

CORNELIA: *(Who doesn't understand.)* Your robe is ready, the dresser's waiting for you in her cubicle.

EMMA: Do you feel it too? *(She opens her arms wide and breathes in the sensation.)* Do you feel it as I do...everywhere in the room.... She touched this table. She sat there. She looked at everything and you'll never guess.... I'm invited to sing at Windsor, in a private recital.

CORNELIA: So me too, I'm.... You'll need an accompanist, no? *(EMMA is taken aback.)*

EMMA: I must go now.

               (She goes to exit, stops, takes a deep breath in surveying the room, and leaves. CORNELIA is left alone, goes to exit in her turn, then stops and opens her arms wide, trying to feel what her sister felt. When nothing happens, she shrugs her shoulders and goes out.

               End of ACT ONE.)

ACT TWO

(We hear the strains of "Lohengrin." The four women, EMMA, CORNELIA, EVA, and the QUEEN are discovered downstage, their faces lit in cameo. During EMMA's first speech the QUEEN begins to nod off.)

EMMA: When I sang for the first time in front of Her Majesty, I performed *Caro nome, Robin Adair, Ave Maria,* Gounod's *Jewel Song, Home Sweet Home,* and three pieces of...Wagner; a selection of melodies that gave the Queen much pleasure. She congratulated me on my voice and interpretation in such a discerning manner that I realized at once she had a sound grasp of music and the art of singing.

(The QUEEN has dozed off, her mouth slack like that of a sleeping child.)

When I finished singing, she remained for a brief moment fixed in a state of reverie.

(The QUEEN wakes up and applauds politely.)

VICTORIA: "To the Crown Princess of Prussia: Pray send me what music is published of the new opera of Wagner—as I admire his operas very much. I should be very grateful if you would send it me—as Beatrice would play it. *Lohengrin* is our great favourite—he was so handsome in his white costume with his armour and helmet, and the beautiful light strongly projected on him seemed to wrap him in a halo. But you mustn't think we're becoming too modern. We love our Gounod every bit as much. His *Faust* is so delightful."

(The light goes out on the QUEEN.)

EVA: Windsor Castle, 8 July 1874. "Sir Thomas Biddulph, at the Queen's comand, presents his compliments to Madame Albani. He is desired by the Queen to ask her to accept the accompanying necklace and cross as a souvenir of her visit to Windsor last week."

CORNELIA: I never went to Windsor.

EVA: You didn't accompany her....

CORNELIA: No. In fact, I've been to very few places. Though I've packed a good many trunks in my time; hers especially. No, I stayed here in London and carried my cross. I haven't seen the world, as they say.

                (She goes to the table and helps herself to a cup of liquid from the teapot; she drinks from the cup.)

                Put that back in its place please. It's not polite to snoop. *(She laughs.)* My sister always believed one could possess the music. We talk about possessing one's instrument, or possessing one's art. Fiddlesticks! It is the art which possesses us. To the very end. That was brought home to me once when a dreadful thing happened at the Met. She was on tour, and the tenor Castlemary missed a note while he was singing in *Martha.* He was finishing his aria when what at first sounded like a variation on the final trill turned into a violent cough. The poor man was holding his arms up to the flies as the village girls danced around him. The audience was laughing and egging him on, so delighted were they by this moment of improvisation. Then he collapsed. And the public broke into thunderous applause.

EVA: Oh, my God...he was....

CORNELIA: Dead, yes. They carried him back to his dressing room and laid him out on the bed, hideously made-up in his fop's costume. The music which had nourished his whole life had taken it from him. Do I frighten you? Enough talk, to work; let's have a look at the Mozart. I trust you comprehend what you're singing.

EVA: I went over the score this morning.

CORNELIA: I see that lip is still swollen. They don't feed you where you're staying? *(She glances down at teacup.)* You must break this dreadful habit. Speak the words of the aria.

EVA: Where are they now, those happy moments of sweetness and pleasure? Where have they flown, those solemn vows made by those lying lips?

CORNELIA: Why does the recollection of that bliss still haunt my breast after destiny snatched it from me?

EVA: Not destiny, mademoiselle, memory...in the text it's "*la memoria.*"

CORNELIA: Quite so, but the text is not betrayed. Destiny and Memory are two sides of the same coin, according to your age or mine. You will draw out, ever so lightly, the *Do, Doooove sono...*

(ERNEST GYE enters surreptitiously, bouquet in hand; only CORNELIA sees him. He resembles his father closely; in fact, the same actor plays both roles.)

CORNELIA: Do you like flowers, Eva?

EVA: I adore them.

CORNELIA: Do you know that my sister once interrupted a performance because the overpowering scent of flowers in her dressing room affected her violently?

EVA: I read that somewhere.

CORNELIA: Of course.

EVA: Too many flowers. What success she must have known.

CORNELIA: Success, when it comes, is always unpredictable, like a storm. If you're unprepared for it, you get soaked. To work now. Mozart!

(ERNEST coughs slightly.)

Ernest, what a lovely surprise! Flowers! You shouldn't

have. Here, let me relieve you. Gladiolas, my favourites.... Oh, but let me look at you.... Goodness, you're so chic...you've just come from your club, no? I wanted to thank you—for last week at Kew Gardens. Such a wonderful stroll.... *(She smiles complicitly.)* Especially towards the end when you agreed to escort me home. Would you care to sit down...some tea?

ERNEST: No.

CORNELIA: *(Her eyes not leaving his.)* I should fetch some water for the flowers. You know that we received a letter from father this morning? He'll be here for the premiere of *The Marriage of Figaro. (A beat.)* What is it, Ernest? Not feeling well? Cat got your tongue? I'll run and find a vase and ask them to make the tea....

ERNEST: The flowers are for Mademoiselle Emma. *(CORNELIA stops dead. She turns to him.)* I have come.... I have come to propose.

CORNELIA: I see. *(A beat.)* What exactly is your proposition?

ERNEST: I beg you, Cornelia, don't make this more difficult than it already is.

CORNELIA: I thought we had an understanding. I thought that last Sunday... *(She approaches him.)* when you kissed me here *(She kisses him on the mouth.)*, I thought that was as good as a promise.

ERNEST: I thought so too.

CORNELIA: What has happened? Why? *(A beat.)* Yes, of course. God the Father, Saint Frederic Gye, our patron saint, sees things differently.

ERNEST: There are many changes at Covent Garden. Immediately after *The Marriage* we leave for the United States. Father has organized an extensive tour.

CORNELIA: After the marriage?

ERNEST: *The Marriage of Figaro.*

CORNELIA: And the other marriage?

ERNEST: Next summer, if all goes well...

CORNELIA: And the bride-to-be is aware of this?

ERNEST: I believe that Father has hinted as much.

CORNELIA: Has hinted as much? How charming. *(Offhandedly.)* My dear Emma, your new costumes have arrived, your latest reviews are excellent and by the way, my son was wondering if you wouldn't care to spend the rest of your life in his bed.

ERNEST: It's a delicate situation for both of us, Cornelia, and for Covent Garden.... Sometimes we have to make compromises.

CORNELIA: Like letting Papa dictate who his youngest will sleep with?

ERNEST: Must you paint such a vulgar picture?

CORNELIA: You think it's pretty? You English are all alike, you decide everything ensconced in your stuffy drawing rooms, teacups delicately poised, you think it's civilized. But make no mistake, Ernest, it's vulgar, it is absolutely vulgar.... When your father talks about your marriage to Emma while sipping his sherry, it's a question of poking, pure and simple. Poking! *(She yells it.)*

ERNEST: Cornelia! You're going to rouse the neighbourhood!

CORNELIA: You'd rather I were silent, dignified and obliging, I suppose. Like those creatures painted on your dessert plates, bathing in cream and upside-down cakes! Well, I will not be silent, Ernest. People are not fools, my sister is not a fool.... Do you really believe she'll stand for that? *(She takes the flowers and gives them to him.)* Go ahead and see! And good luck. Emma knows very well what I feel for you...since that first day in your father's...excuse me, God the Father's office.

ERNEST: Cornelia, it was apparently your sister's idea. She told Father it would be wise to consolidate her association with Covent Garden through its future director. That it would be the surest means of discouraging any temptation to consider more enticing offers from a rival house. As was the case with Madame Patti. Your sister is a great artist, Cornelia. She also has a talent for managing her career.

CORNELIA: You talk of my sister, of your father, but you, your voice...I don't hear your voice, Ernest.... But it was you last month at Ascot, it was you in the open cab last Sunday, not your father...you and me.... Not your father, not Emma, just you and me.... *I'm* the one you took in your arms....

             (We hear EVA practising her scales.)

             Emma, who rehearses the lives of others, whilst I struggle only to live my own. It's too absurd.

ERNEST: You're very upset. Sit down, Cornelia.

CORNELIA: I shall sit on the love seat, isn't that what you call it? *(A beat.)* I must thank you, Ernest.

ERNEST: But....

CORNELIA: I say it without irony. You have made me very happy...really.... All those hours, all those precious seconds when I thought, it's here, it's him, he's the one, all those weeks waiting for the good weather so we could go out in the carriage together, I've been more than happy, I've lived in hope, the first real hope I've felt since leaving Canada.... It's made me think of when I was little, when kindness was a benchmark of sorts.... "Be kind"...and if I was kind, all my hopes would be fulfilled.... I'm so awkward in society, I find it so terrifying. That's the difficulty, isn't it?

ERNEST: Father says that above all an opera director's wife must be a diplomat.

CORNELIA: A diplomat. Of course. When I go into a stranger's house it's like I'm entering another country. I tell myself, you've got to be witty, find something, be scintillating, polish those rough edges, make yourself interesting like the others.... People are so vile to one another. *Cosi fan tutte.* Be kind.... "She's awfully kind, isn't she, she couldn't be nicer".... Once upon a time that was enough. *(She looks at ERNEST and realizes he doesn't understand.)* It's all right, Ernest, you can't understand. In any case, I'd never make a presentable wife. You will have the direction of Covent Garden, and...I shall doubtless make a lovely maid of honour.

> *(One must be aware, seeing the two of them seated together on the sofa, that what is happening to them has nothing to do with their real wishes. As they listen to the aria, they regard each other sadly, like people who love each other, but must remain apart in public. We hear and see EVA, in the throes of her lesson, singing the Countess's aria, "Dove sono," from "The Marriage of Figaro." The following exchange occurs before the beginning of the second verse.)*

CORNELIA: I should be singing that. If I had a voice.

ERNEST: I'm sorry.

CORNELIA: If I had a voice.

ERNEST: You have a voice.

CORNELIA: Yes, but not the kind one hears, or listens to.

> *(They are silent during the second verse of the aria, and CORNELIA is back in her lesson. At the end she is in tears, disconcerted, undone. ERNEST, in the shade, remains seated at her side. Meanwhile EMMA has entered.)*

CORNELIA: *(To EVA.)* **That will be all for today. I'm afraid Mozart undoes me.**

> *(EVA passes her a handkerchief, and ERNEST does the same. She takes ERNEST's.)*

EVA: *(Moved.)* **I'm so sorry, I didn't know.**

CORNELIA: Emma, there are some flowers for you on the table, and I believe Ernest has something to ask you.

EVA: **Next week, then, Mademoiselle.**

> *(EVA exits, followed by CORNELIA.)*

EMMA: You've told her.

ERNEST: It had to be done.

EMMA: Cornelia is strong. She'll recover quickly.

ERNEST: I wish it could have happened differently. *(A beat.)* She looked so unhappy..

EMMA: Cornelia has little talent for happiness. A pity, because she has almost all the others. Ernest, don't look at me like that, please, it's hard for all of us. Someone has to bear the brunt of it, however. Me. Such is the price of Art. Shall we get on with it, then? It was the right decision, yes, the right decision. *(She kisses him on the cheek without any real affection.)* The itinerary for the tour, has it come? Do we go to Montreal?

ERNEST: Emma, it's not the tour that has brought me here.

EMMA: You're not seriously thinking of proposing.... No, that would be absurd...we've discussed it and it's fine with me...no need to clutter it with romance.

ERNEST: I'd feel much happier if we could do it according to form.

EMMA: Very well, but not here. Cornelia tells me Kew Gardens is the ideal location for an amorous stroll; take me there next Sunday and we'll have all the time in the world to discuss it....

ERNEST: Emma, do you love me? I mean, have you any real feeling for me? Father told me....

EMMA: I have many feelings for your father, Ernest, if I may borrow your phrase. Things have happened so quickly, and you and I scarcely know one another.... We will have a lifetime to remedy that. Don't be in a rush. Your father is a genius to put you in charge of the company tour. Clearly his plans are well settled for us. Has he ever been wrong?

ERNEST: No. At least, not with me. And evidently not with you either. You take his side with such passion.

EMMA: I love your father a great deal. It's as simple as that. I came from the back woods and he gave me London.

ERNEST: You're prepared to marry me just to thank him? If you feel nothing for me, isn't that rather a high price to pay?

EMMA: Do you realize the successive generations it took, Mr Gye, living quietly, far from your cities, and breathing a purer air, to beget health, perfect lungs, a voice? Great artists benefit from the wisdom of their ancestors. I inherited the lassitude of my grandmothers, spinning patiently before their fires. My voice comes out of their silence. *(A beat.)* My marriage with you will permit me to thank the entire world. We shall learn to love one another.

ERNEST: *(A beat, then, coming to life.)* We go to New York, Salt Lake City, San Francisco, Chicago...Toronto, Quebec and Montreal...and other cities along the way.... That's the itinerary, more or less.... We shall leave immediately after *The Marriage*, I mean, the *Figaro*.

EMMA: Now I recognize you. There, that's the old Ernest for whom...I have feelings. *(She smiles.)*

ERNEST: Will Cornelia make the trip?

EMMA: No.

ERNEST: She'll be disappointed. She was so looking forward to returning to Canada..

EMMA: Given the circumstances, I think it would be cruel to take her with us. The voyage will be exhausting, and if, besides working very hard, we are busy...taming one another, so to speak, her presence would be intolerable. She needs a period of separation, as they say. I know all too well how she feels towards you.

ERNEST: Cornelia and I have never....

EMMA: Spare me, please, I don't wish to know. It would be like listening at the keyhole. In any case, your father has found her a post. She's to teach music to the King of Spain's children.

ERNEST: But Cornelia doesn't know a word of Spanish!

EMMA: And the King of Spain's children not one note of music. She'll have her work cut out for her.

ERNEST: *(Astonished.)* Evidently. Everything's running so ship-shape, one only has to ride the waves. And the rehearsals for *Figaro*?

EMMA: The rehearsals are going splendidly, but I'm a bit nervous. The opera has so many sopranos, sometimes it feels like a horse-race. Mozart's a nightmare for performers. Still, for those who work hard, the rewards are great. Certain critics will perhaps be kind enough to call it a triumph. We could certainly do with one. *Lohengrin* went well enough, but the British public has yet to develop an ear for the Germans. With the Italians it's so much less risky.

ERNEST: Perhaps someday an Englishman will compose an opera of worth.

EMMA: Don't be absurd, the English don't know how to talk about love. *(She realizes what she has just said.)* Forgive me, I meant no offence. What I meant is that the English lack the facility of the Italians.

ERNEST: And Canadians, can they talk about love?

EMMA: Canadians have an average of ten to twelve children, and spend their summers getting ready for the cold. They haven't time to talk about love. When I think about it, I can't see, I can no longer see, how I could ever live there. I'm English now. Not actually, of course; but nonetheless, English.

ERNEST: But when you think of your country.... Aren't we all a touch patriotic?

EMMA: I am an artist. Art is a country unto itself. Not open to all who wish to enter. I must return for my warm-up. Pray excuse me. Tonight is our last *Mignon*, Thursday next the premiere of *Figaro*, and then the tour. *(She heads for the door, then turns.)* Oh, I was forgetting.... *(She approaches him and points to her cheek. He kisses it.)* Off you go, now. *(She moves to exit, stops again and turns.)* Isn't it a remarkable thing, Destiny?

(They go their separate ways. CORNELIA appears. It is evident she has heard the entire scene. With reddened eyes she comes forward and picks up the

flowers that EMMA has not touched. She looks at the audience. We hear a crescendo of noisy and ongoing applause. Royal Albert Hall, 14 October 1911. The farewell concert, from the wings, EMMA enters.)

CORNELIA: They want you back again.

EMMA: They want me to leave. Well, let them wait.

CORNELIA: Go on, now...what's the matter with you?

EMMA: No, let them stew for a bit.... *(She listens.)* There, now's the moment...here we go...this is how you take your bows.

(She leaves, smiling as soon as she enters the light. The applause redoubles. Fade out of the lights, sound of the applause, and EMMA. The piano in the room where CORNELIA is giving her lesson is now practically bare. Gone are the picture frames, the collection of eggs.)

EVA: **The Royal Albert Hall was full?**

CORNELIA: *(Holding one of her famous cups of tea, and a bit tipsy.)* **Many of the seats were complimentary. But they were all there: Charles Sanford, Edward Elgar, Mathilde Marchesi. All the queens of opera and song, Adelina Patti, Emma Calvé....**

EVA: **Nellie Melba?**

CORNELIA: **La Melba was there. In a vast canary-yellow dress.** *(They laugh.)* **Like Anne Boleyn at Catherine of Aragon's funeral.**

EVA: **And the King?**

CORNELIA: **We have nothing to do with royalty now.** *(A beat, then, totally engrossed in her thought.)* **That evening they were whistling for her, begging for an encore! If you could have seen her, mademoiselle, her eyes full of real tears! How could they deny the daughter of Bellini one last song?**

(EMMA returns, her arms laden with bouquets, and gives the overflow to CORNELIA.)

EMMA: Here, take these…. *(She exits again.)*

CORNELIA: *(To EVA.)* **Bringing me flowers was very thoughtful.**

EVA: **You were so sad last week.**

CORNELIA: **A bad day. They're magnificent. I'm so touched.**

EVA: **They're Madame Albani's favourite flowers.** *(CORNELIA freezes.)* **I read that somewhere. Might I be able to see her today?**

CORNELIA: *(Her mood completely altered.)* **An obsession.**

EVA: **Is she here?**

CORNELIA: *(Coldly.)* **What about your homework? Did you review the Handel I lent you?**

EVA: **The thing is…**

CORNELIA: **Yes?**

EVA: **I meant to tell you…**

CORNELIA: **Yes?**

EVA: **I mislaid the scores in a railway station. King's Cross, I believe.**

CORNELIA: *(Stung.)* **Mislaid. Really? They were expensive, you'll have to replace them. You can go to Chappell's on Wigmore Street. In the meantime, take this. One of your predecessors left it behind. A remarkably gifted girl. What talent she had!**

EVA: *Tosca?* **You can't be serious. It's not at all right for me.**

CORNELIA: **Allow me to be the judge of that.**

EVA: **Tosca's a dramatic soprano. I'll ruin my voice…**

CORNELIA: **Prima donna! Fuss, fuss, fuss! Obviously you'll never sing the role, it takes stomach to sing Tosca, but it's ideal for stretching the voice…. Now, take your place….**

EVA: **Mademoiselle Cornelia, I'm going to damage my voice!**

CORNELIA: **Fiddlesticks.**

EVA: **I haven't done my scales yet.**

CORNELIA: **No matter, you hate doing them anyway. Pay attention to your attack.... *VIIIIiisssi D'AAARRRRTE, Andante lento appasionato....* Love and Music, for you only have I lived. All set?**

EVA: **But....**

CORNELIA: *(Ignoring her.)* **Ready? Now, bite into those words.**

EVA: **Mademoiselle Corn...**

CORNELIA: **The words, I said, not your lips!**

(EVA sings "Vissi d'arte, vissi d'amore," from Puccini's "Tosca." It is important that she not quite make it when she comes to "sempre con fe sincera diedi fiori agl'altar.")

(Yelling at her pupil.) **Diedi fiori agl'altar... Fiori! Flowers, like those you brought for my sister, it's not that difficult...**

(Unable to bear her teacher's harshness, EVA grabs her handbag and runs off in tears.)

Eva, come back! *(She grabs her cane and runs after her.)*

(1888, Scotland. Old Mar Lodge. A rural atmosphere. QUEEN VICTORIA and EMMA will take tea in the summer residence of Madame Albani. Furniture made from cane or of fine wood from the colonies, or the suggestion of such.

QUEEN VICTORIA enters unobtrusively, delighted to discover she is alone. She sits, and assumes the attitude of waiting for something, we know not what. Nothing happens. We feel her impatience; everyday, as opposed to royal, impatience. She rises and approaches the piano, finding there the score of Sir

Henry Bishop's "Home Sweet Home," words by John Howard Payne. She casts a look around her, rather like a thief about to steal something, then sits at the piano. She looks at the score very closely and begins to play. It is an absolute disaster. She massacres the music, interspersing it with false notes, filling it with the most discordant harmonies. All the time she is playing, she smiles with satisfaction. After a moment or two we hear coming from off somewhere:)

CORNELIA: Frederic! Frederic! Get down from the piano this instant! I've told you a hundred times, it is not a toy! Your mother doesn't want you picking at it. Freeeederic!

(CORNELIA appears and discovers the QUEEN.)

Oh, Your Majesty! *(She curtsies.)*

VICTORIA: Is it not a remarkable melody? *(She continues for a moment, then stops.)* If you only knew how I envy you, Mademoiselle Cornelia. Music. To live with Music! Sometimes I indulge in a little reverie, and I imagine myself like you, simple and happy, without all the dreadful responsibilities of Empire.... Not bad for a Sunday pianist, no? My hands are so stiff.... Time is a god, and there's no escaping him.... But I can always sign my documents and give the royal greeting. *(She waves with her hand.)* That's all that matters! *(A beat.)* Mademoiselle Cornelia, I should like to ask a favour...I realize it may seem odd to you.... *(With energy.)* I want you to do something for me.

CORNELIA: Whatever Your Majesty desires.

VICTORIA: Good. Tell me what happens.

CORNELIA: Your Majesty?

VICTORIA: Yes, yes, tell me...the home of an artist.... It's why I always accept your sister's invitations, you see. Out of curiosity. I make up a story. I imagine myself one of my own subjects, visiting the home of the great Albani. For example, before playing this wonderful page of music, I fancied myself in the waiting room of a train station.... I have never waited for a train, do you know that? The train is always on time when I take it. There are so many things that I've never done...But pray, tell me, how do you spend your days?

CORNELIA: Your Majesty, I'd be too afraid to bore you with my affairs, and I...

VICTORIA: Not the least in the world, it is I who am asking you. The morning, for example...

CORNELIA: Here, Your Majesty?

VICTORIA: No, no, in town. This is the country, this is Scotland.

CORNELIA: The morning? I get up very early, Your Majesty. As soon as I'm out of bed I go down to the kitchen and see to the breakfast of Mr Gye and Emma, the upkeep of the house, and I try to solve everyone's little problems.

VICTORIA: Like me. Pray, what does Albani eat?

CORNELIA: *(Astonished by the oddness of the question.)* That depends on the day, Your Majesty. Scrambled eggs sometimes, poached eggs...

VICTORIA: Delightful. With just a hint of curry. How divine! Continue.

CORNELIA: Once breakfast is over, I give out the day's tasks: waxing the floors, cleaning the windows, filling the lamps, polishing the silver...

VICTORIA: Polishing the silver? Whatever for?

CORNELIA: Silver tarnishes, Your Majesty, you have to rub it to restore its brilliance, otherwise it goes black.

VICTORIA: *(A long beat, during which she struggles to understand; then, very intrigued.)* Yes...well, of course.

CORNELIA: The rest of the morning is devoted to correspondence. After that a light meal, a walk in the afternoon, a visit to the milliner or dressmaker, and then it's teatime. I buy the evening paper and read out the headlines for Emma and Mr Gye before they go off to the theatre.

VICTORIA: What, you don't go with them?

CORNELIA: I go for the premieres, but as you know, Ma'am, there are fewer and fewer since the financial worries of the last years, and in any case, I have a great deal of work to do. I prepare my lessons.

VICTORIA: They told me you had left your post at the Royal House of Spain.

CORNELIA: *(A beat.)* It was suggested that my services were no longer required.

VICTORIA: Why is that, pray?

CORNELIA: The prince traded his piano for a pastime more befitting his years. I gave up my post with much relief, Your Majesty. I have more than enough to keep me occupied with my sister's son and my private pupils.

VICTORIA: So predictable, children.... And your sister, what does she do while you are moving heaven and earth to keep her house in order?

CORNELIA: Your Majesty is surely aware of the terrible price a singer pays to belong to Covent Garden's first family.

VICTORIA: Do I detect a hint of irony, or is that something you've learned by rote?

CORNELIA: Everyone pays a price, Your Majesty. At least, that's what I believe.

VICTORIA: I never thought I'd talk philosophy today.

CORNELIA: I beg pardon, Ma'am.

VICTORIA: *(With great compassion.)* It's three summers now that you've been coming to Balmoral, Mademoiselle Cornelia, and each time I see you I have the feeling it's not you in front of me, but an image of you. It's as if there's another country in your eyes, but far, very far away. And you inhabit this country, while the rest of us are excluded. Regret.... You were a musician in your own right, were you not?

CORNELIA: I was a musician, but music didn't take to me. I say it without bitterness. It's true, I used to dream of being a concert artist. I ended up instead with an orchestra of pots and pans and an army of floor polishers. Her Majesty understands, I'm not complaining. My sister is simply "up there," and I hold the ladder. For there to be an Albani, there must be a hundred women like me.

(The QUEEN touches CORNELIA with great sympathy. EMMA comes in, carrying a tea tray.)

EMMA: The staff are all busy with dinner, Your Majesty, so we shall do our own tea.

VICTORIA: How splendid. I've been having such a delightful conversation with your sister; she's a woman with many secrets, who often reminds me of myself. *(She smiles at CORNELIA.)*

(A long silence ensues, during which the QUEEN is caught up in her reflections. EMMA looks at CORNELIA with vexation. CORNELIA makes signals to her to do something, which EMMA fails to comprehend. CORNELIA mimes the action of playing the piano. EMMA rises and goes to it.)

EMMA: Oh! *Home Sweet Home!* What a pretty song. Would Your Majesty care to hear it? *(The QUEEN appears to be elsewhere.)* Would Her Majesty like me to sing for her while Cornelia pours the tea?

VICTORIA: You know, Cornelia, you are right. For a Victoria, there must be thousands of other women. *(EMMA remains at the piano, irked by a feeling of exclusion.)* Is the great Albani going to sing for me, or ought we to wait until after tea?

EMMA: I should be honoured, Your Majesty.

CORNELIA: Her Majesty will take her tea now?

VICTORIA: Yes, now. *(She looks at EMMA.)* Now.

(CORNELIA is at the tea table, busying herself with the QUEEN's cup. As EMMA starts to play the introduction, she is visibly irritated by the noise her sister is making with the spoon and saucer. She is

*about to launch into the song, her mouth open, when
a fresh clatter of china arrests her inspiration. In a
tempo too rapid and with ill-humour, she then
repeats the introduction.)*

No, no, that's much too fast. It's *Home Sweet Home*, isn't
it? I shouldn't fancy being in a home like the one you're
playing. It's like a military march. Start again. Now, for
a *Home Sweet Home* a little more English.

(EMMA is furious.)

EMMA: Perhaps Cornelia ought to accompany me after all.

VICTORIA: That would be delightful.

*(CORNELIA goes to join her at the piano—and it is
clearly EVA who will sing as they return to the
lesson.)*

EVA: **You asked me to come back; you promised me I could
see her if I returned to my lessons...**

CORNELIA: **She's with people more important than you and I this
morning.**

EVA: **At this rate she could die twenty times before I'll get
to meet her.**

CORNELIA: **Time is on your side. Be patient. A prima donna dies
three deaths: when her beauty fades, when her voice
fails, and when the breath leaves the body. Albani is
dying her second death, and it's a prolonged agony.
You will see her. You know the score by heart?**

EMMA: *(To CORNELIA.)* When you're ready.

CORNELIA: *(To EVA.)* **It was one of Queen Victoria's favourite
songs. When you're ready.**

VICTORIA: *(To EVA.)* But very gently, pray. Like a summer breeze.

EMMA: Very well, Your Majesty.

*(CORNELIA launches into the song, this time with
soul, and EVA sings it through. While she sings, the
QUEEN will fall into a deep sleep as was often the
case in her later years.*

Song: "Home Sweet Home."

EVA finishes the song with satisfaction, and once the last note has sounded we hear a light snoring from the QUEEN, which stops after a moment. She wakes with a start.)

VICTORIA: Charming! I could listen to you for hours, Madame Albani, it's so restful.

(She takes a sip of her tea and her face lights up; she takes a second mouthful, then a third.)

Mmmm...this tea is de-lec-ta-ble...a clever mixture of...Mademoiselle Cornelia, what did you put in it to give it this slight taste of whisky?

CORNELIA: Whisky, Your Majesty.

VICTORIA: How wonderful! *(She laughs.)* You are...very special, my dear, do you know that? With certain people that would be such bad form, but with you it is utterly charming. You have something else as well...you have *le sens de la fête*, a real *sens de la fête*.
The Royal House of Spain made a grave error when they let you go, but once again those Spaniards prove themselves...

(She stops suddenly and shifts slightly in her seat as if some strange phenomenon were taking place inside her. One must appreciate that even queens have anatomical requirements.)

You must excuse me, I'm a trifle weary. The Queen will see you again at dinner.

(She exits with elegance, but with a surprising urgency for a woman her age. The two sisters are alone.)

EMMA: Was it something I said? Where do you suppose she's off to?

CORNELIA: The other throne. *(A beat.)* Go on.

EMMA: What?

CORNELIA: Spit it out. Let's have a scene. I'm ready.

EMMA: I've no wish to have a scene.

              (CORNELIA goes to the table and pours a large whisky into her cup.)

EMMA: You might at least put it in a glass.

CORNELIA: I prefer my whisky in a cup. And so does the Queen of England. Half and half. Why else would the British concoct a drink the same colour as tea?

EMMA: You and your *sens de la fête*! How dare you tell her you were discharged from the Spanish court?

CORNELIA: She knew.

EMMA: She knew? Oh, my God.

CORNELIA: That woman has her eye on every royal house in Europe. She feigns ignorance, but if you look closely in the corner of her eye, you can tell she knows everything, that she enjoys the spectacle, the spectacle of ordinary people thrashing about like fish out of water, trying to save face.

EMMA: You're speaking of the most powerful woman in the world as if you were at school together.

CORNELIA: She's a woman, Emma, like us.

EMMA: She's a Queen, and you should speak to her like a queen.

CORNELIA: She's a woman, and I will speak to her like a woman. That makes your blood boil, eh? That your bosom friend and I talk together like charladies.... Look at yourself. An eel, writhing in pain over hot coals, cooking to the bone. Pathetic!

EMMA: I won't listen to your intemperate ravings one minute further.... *(She gets up to leave.)*

CORNELIA: She knows everything! She knows that since the death of God the Father, Covent Garden has a hole in its pocket. That we're saddled with debts, that once again you're obliged to take to the road to fill up the piggybank. She knows exactly what went on at the Royal House of Spain.

To the Queen! *(She drinks and pours herself another cup.)*

EMMA: I forbid you to take another drop!

CORNELIA: Who's going to stop me?

EMMA: The servants will talk.

CORNELIA: The servants like it more than I do.

EMMA: You could at least wait till the proper hour. It's not even six.

CORNELIA: I've spent twenty years waiting for the proper hour, Emma. I told myself that in the end it would come, that things would be better in a week, a month, a year. Twenty years I've been waiting, twenty years I've had a country lodged in my throat, Emma, *my* country. All that time I've looked after your home, brought up your son and cared for your husband, who properly should have been mine. Until one day I said to myself, you're mistaken, Cornelia, your time will never come. It's pointless to wait for it, it's already here, your time. Do you understand?

               All those years I was waiting for my life to begin...well, that *was* my life!

               This is not one of your operas, Emma. There's no dress rehearsal for life. Life is here, now. It's now that I'm thirsty. It's now that I drink.

EMMA: Cornelia, I beg you...the Queen is here, in our home. I don't want you saying whatever you like at dinner.

CORNELIA: And I don't wish to dine with you. I'm not hungry...in fact, do you know what I want...really want...I want a man. Does that shock you? But my poor Emma, these things you already know. I've slept with lots of men, and not just anybody, good people...very, very, very good people. At one time, even, I was known as "the prince's thoroughfare."

EMMA: There's no end to your obscenities. I've laid everything before you, you've had everything you ever needed to live an extraordinary life, and look what you've done with it.

CORNELIA: It's true, I lost my job at the Royal House of Spain because I slept with the secretary…. They know it, the Queen knows it, you know it, and I know it…why pretend otherwise.

EMMA: There are some things that are just not done. *(She grabs her by the arm.)* Don't you believe in anything?

CORNELIA: I don't believe in things I don't have. Your idea of my "extraordinary" life, I have to get rid of it, it drives me to despair! I don't hear applause every time I open my mouth; no one asks me to scribble my name on a programme; I haven't travelled the world like you, but there's not a place my soul hasn't travelled, and that, Emma, that's because I have one…a soul. Do you remember your own, the one you lost? Perhaps it was that day you looked into the Thames and gazed at your reflection, the very day you began to believe you were English.

EMMA: You think I had a choice, you dimwitted goose? You think it was in my power to do otherwise? I received a gift, more than a gift, a favour was bestowed on me, an obligation. I never asked for it, I was granted it. And the responsibility it conferred on me to become a great artist was beyond sacrifice, just as it's beyond your understanding.

            I belong to England now, I belong to the world, do you hear, and no French Canadian amateur can tell me otherwise!

CORNELIA: I don't believe in you anymore. I believe in chaos, grief, misery, despair, the filth in the streets of London! I need alcohol, tears, coarse laughter, the earth under my feet, mud…. I believe in the life I have. Not the one you promised me.

EMMA: If you want to go back to Canada, plant your feet in the snow and drink with a bunch of peasants, go right ahead, no one's stopping you. I've opened all the doors, you've met dozens of potential husbands, and each time you've resisted because Madame apparently has a soul, a sooooul, and Madame believes in the earth and the mud.

Very well then, go back to the earth, go back to the mud! But I, I shall never let myself be dragged into your mud.... Pack your bags and get out.... *(CORNELIA goes to help herself again.)* You only want to spoil everything....

(EMMA tries to prevent her. They struggle together, almost like the little girls they once were. ERNEST enters without knocking.)

ERNEST: Sherry-time?

CORNELIA: Is it time now, Emma?

ERNEST: Emma insists that sherry be drunk at six. Not before.

EMMA: The public likes performances to begin on time. Not before.

ERNEST: I'm not disturbing you?

EMMA: On the contrary, we were just chatting.

CORNELIA: On the contrary, Emma was making a scene. In fact, not a scene, the scene. It's always the same, isn't it, Emma? Indignation at first, then shouting, some threats, and finally the pardon. We had reached the threats. I believe I've just been dismissed.

(She goes out, repressing a giggle. A beat.)

ERNEST: A shower?

EMMA: A storm...Ernest?

ERNEST: Hmm?

EMMA: Do I have a soul?

ERNEST: Well...uh...

EMMA: Answer me, do I have a soul?

ERNEST: Emma, you're trembling! I know you're thinking about the autumn and you're anxious. Such a perfectionist, do

I have a soul! Look, it's a simple enough score, no major difficulties. You'll be an extraordinary Marguerite.

EMMA: They say I'm a faultless technician, but that I lack soul. Do you believe that?

ERNEST: Who's they?

EMMA: Surely to God it's not so difficult to tell!

ERNEST: Yes. Of course you have a soul. Think of all the charity concerts you give. You have a great soul. A generous soul.

EMMA: Yes. That's true.

ERNEST: Those who say you have no soul are just jealous.

(He sits close to her.)

EMMA: You stink.

ERNEST: My watch must be fast. *(Playful.)* Shall I tell you a secret, madame? I love your soul well enough, but I've a passion for everything that guards it. *(He kisses her on the neck, then on the mouth. Caressing her.)* Is your soul hidden here, or here, or perhaps here? Ah-ha, I believe it's here! *(He buries his head in her breasts.)*

EMMA: I have a soul. I have a soul.

(EVA sings "Connais-tu le pays?" from the opera "Mignon" by Ambroise Thomas. All through the sung portion we must be aware of an uneasiness in CORNELIA. She senses that something is not quite right with her young pupil. Towards the end of the piece she stops her.)

EVA: **Something wrong? Am I too slow?**

CORNELIA: *(Observing her.)* **No. You're singing extremely well. Your progress is astounding.** *(A beat.)* **But you have the look of someone who's cheated at cards. You're late with your payments, two lessons in fact. Why is that? It's something you should be careful about, money. "*Quando la miseria entra dalla porta, l'amore se ne va dalla finestra,*" as they say in Italy. When** poverty knocks at the door, love runs out through the window. What's the matter?

EVA: This is my last lesson. I won't be coming back.

CORNELIA: I see. And who is it?

EVA: What?

CORNELIA: You've found a new teacher, less traditional, more in vogue?

EVA: I'm going home. To Canada. I don't like it here. I don't belong. *(A beat.)* I'm not happy.

CORNELIA: My dear child, here is where it will happen. There are days when we all feel homesick. It doesn't last.

EVA: Really?

CORNELIA: You are prepared to sacrifice two years of effort on this sudden whim?

EVA: Don't worry, I'll pay for the six remaining lessons.

CORNELIA: That's not in question. You have a tremendous talent, great things await you here. It would be such a waste to go back.

EVA: To sing *Traviata* in Montreal or London, it's still to sing *Traviata*. I want to sing for my own people.

CORNELIA: But the best season of your life is about to begin!

EVA: Back home we also have a spring, Mademoiselle Cornelia. Have you forgotten?

CORNELIA: *(A beat.)* No, I never forgot. Though I tried to.

EVA: Why did you never go back?

(1910. London. Tregunter Road. A drawing room. EMMA enters in high turmoil, her arms loaded with costumes. CORNELIA is in excellent spirits.)

EMMA: It's no use. They're not interested in anything. The man in Drury Lane explained to me that the world of opera is redefining itself aesthetically, and that my costumes are from a bygone era. He advised me to wait, that perhaps a museum would be interested. A museum! They're stale, he said. I only wore Isolde's costume four times. Four times!

CORNELIA: We can make curtains from the capes.

EMMA: Ernest is still in bed?

CORNELIA: I haven't seen him yet this morning.

EMMA: He was spitting all night long. What are we going to do? I couldn't insist, they could tell. I felt like a beggar. I showed them everything, role by role; for every opera I had a juicy anecdote. They were amused all right; one of the clerks asked me to sign his libretto, his father used to rave about Albani. I'm not even sure we'll be able to pay the servants at the end of the month. We're ruined, Cornelia.

CORNELIA: We?

EMMA: I won't be able to pay you either.

CORNELIA: You can borrow.

EMMA: Cornelia, I'm not about to ask for charity from a bank.

CORNELIA: Clearly you've never been in a bank, charity is the least of their concerns. You can sell the house.

EMMA: Sell! And live where?

CORNELIA: In something more modest. In any case, we're hardly overrun with visitors.

EMMA: Ernest will never agree to sell the house.

CORNELIA: Ernest's incapable of making a decision. Ernest can't even decide how he takes his coffee. Anyway, who wants a house like this?

EMMA: I love this house. It's my haven.

CORNELIA: What colour are the curtains in the upstairs drawing room?

EMMA: Green.

CORNELIA: Blue. Royal blue.

EMMA: My son loves this house.

CORNELIA: Frederic hasn't lived here for a year and never comes to see us. No doubt he lost the address. You might as well send him a new one.

EMMA: We could always take to the road again. Williamson thinks a farewell tour to Australia and South Africa might be lucrative.

CORNELIA: Three times the trick with the hanky? Isn't that overdoing it?

EMMA: There's talk of an oratorio season this winter. (*A beat.*) They're giving another *Figaro* at Covent Garden, perhaps there'll be something for me.

CORNELIA: Perhaps not. The music is demanding.

EMMA: Just what does that mean, the music is demanding? Need I remind you that I was the first to sing Wagner in this country?

CORNELIA: You don't need to, I was there. I'm only suggesting that perhaps it's time to turn the page.

EMMA: wol hours after my death, I'll still be singing.

CORNELIA: (*Gently.*) If you like. At least nobody's ears will be offended. For the last three years, Emma, you've had a frog in your throat. It was charming at first, he was hardly more than a tadpole. But look how he's grown, how he hops all over your vocal chords. He's become a monster, treacherous, unpredicatable, liable to croak in the middle of any song. That frog is called age. You have to know when to go. You can weep, rage, spit in my face; whatever you do, your voice won't come back. Ernest won't tell you, your superhuman efforts have guaranteed him a comfy life. Williamson won't tell you, he can turn a handsome profit in the Cape, in Australia. Your colleagues won't tell you, because when a rival loses her voice, they experience an odd kind of pleasure. Believe me, it's better to say farewell for good before someone asks, "Were you present at the recent recital of Emma Albani, bass-baritone?"

EMMA: I sang for all the crowned heads of Europe, I gave recitals during…

CORNELIA: I sang, I gave. Are you able to accept what's happening to you in the present? Prepare a final recital, invite everyone, and celebrate forty years of song.

EMMA: This house is filled with mementos, testimonials…

CORNELIA: We've sold all the mementos received from the great ones of this world, and all that's left are the ones nobody wants. The ones that are here. *(She points to her temple.)*

               (EMMA rises and goes to the Victrola, puts on a record. It is her own recording of "Ombra mai fu." She is deeply upset. After listening to some of it, she snatches the record from the machine.)

EMMA: Just as I was beginning to understand what music was, just when I was beginning…. I love this life. I love to wander in the wings before a concert, listening to the first stirrings of the public, slowly increasing as the hall fills up. That sound, that too is music. And money? Where are we going to find it?

CORNELIA: *(Glancing at EVA.)* Lessons. We can give lessons.

EMMA: But you've gone completely mad. Singing lessons. Cornelia!

CORNELIA: There's another possibility. Looking over your most recent notes, I found something surprising. Wait, let me find it…. Ah, here it is…. "Early in 1903 I paid my last visit to my beloved Canada." Since the book's not finished, we could still add a chapter.

EMMA: What, go to Canada?

CORNELIA: Yes, go home.

EMMA: And do what?

CORNELIA: The same as here; but for our own people.

EMMA: *(Restraining her anger.)* Our people? What are you talking about? If they were really ours, wouldn't they have done everything to keep us? They should have built opera houses, conservatories, concert halls, our people!

CORNELIA: They have all that now.

EMMA: I don't want to go back. I'm not of the same race as those people. I'm afraid, Cornelia, do you understand.... It's worse than butterflies before a concert, it's a giant insect in my stomach that fills me with terror. I'm afraid I'll have to go back, and I'd never have the courage. It would be like admitting defeat.

CORNELIA: Calm yourself. We'll find a way.

EMMA: I don't want you to go either. I need you. Promise me you won't go.

EVA: **Did you want to go back?**

CORNELIA: **Do I know? Yes and no. The question is futile.** *(A beat.)* I'm going to give lessons. You will help me. We shall invent a method. The Albani method.

EMMA: Has it come to this?

CORNELIA: It's called facing the music.

EMMA: *(She places her hands on her throat.)* A farewell recital. Cornelia, you really think I could?

CORNELIA: Shhh...You don't want to waken the sleeping frog. *(With a costume from Wagner tucked beneath her arm, EMMA goes to exit.)* Two young girls on the bridge of a ship. I remember.

EMMA: Look at us. Look what I've made of you.... The waste.... In those days I never thought, never realized.... Ambition, the need to become someone else had taken up all the room.... But now...now that my voice is going— there, I've said it—now that my voice is leaving me.... I understand at last all that's happened.... I'm sorry, Cornelia.

I cannot forgive myself for letting you play such a thankless role. It kills me.

But you must also know...I cannot forgive you for having agreed to play it.

(She goes out. CORNELIA is still for a moment, then smiles at EVA. We return to the lesson.)

CORNELIA: **Why did we never go back? Simple decency forbid it. We couldn't play the prodigal children when what kept us away was contempt for our roots. You don't spit in your mother's face. There are some things that are just not done.**

I don't know if your decision is right, but I believe your intentions are.

I shall miss you. And you will miss me. *(They are both moved.)* **Do me a kindness.**

EVA: **Yes?**

CORNELIA: **Stop biting your lip. It's unbearable.**

(EVA laughs. We hear the opening strains of EMMA's recording of Handel's "Ombra mai fu." EMMA, draped in one of her old stage costumes, enters and sees EVA in the present time. Realizing she is interrupting the lesson....)

EMMA: **Oh.... I beg your pardon....** *(She goes out.)*

EVA: **Was that...it's....**

CORNELIA: **Albani.**

EVA: **She who sings more sweetly than the birds.**

CORNELIA: **A great voice. A magnificent voice.**

Now we shall end the lesson. Never believe those who speak of the golden age of music, those who claim that everything was better before. Art has no need of those who long for the past. They only get in its way.

(She goes to the piano, and speaks rhetorically to cover her emotion.)

The human voice in relation to music is like a light trained on an object. Each artist illuminates the same work, the same object, differently.

And we need the light so badly.

> *(EVA completes the aria, "Ombra mai fu" full in her own voice.*
>
> *The End.)*

Emma Albani Lajeunesse

A selection of significant dates

1847	Emma born in Chambly, Québec, to musician parents
1856	Emma's first public performance, Mechanic's Hall, Montreal
1860	Emma sings for the Prince of Wales during his tour of Canada
1864	Emma's family moves to Albany, New York, where her father finds work
1868	Emma and Cornelia sail for Europe
1872	Emma Albani makes her Covent Garden operatic debut in *La Sonnambula*
1873	Emma sings for Queen Victoria
1874	Emma triumphs in New York City
1880	Emma debuts in *La Scala* in Milan, one of her rare disasters
1883	Emma debuts in Chicago in *I Puritani*; she returns to Québec after an absence of two decades, and 10,000 people meet her at the station
1885	Emma sings for an audience of 22,000 at the Crystal Palace, London
1891	Emma debuts at the Metropolitan Opera, New York
1896	Emma, in her final Covent Garden season, sings *Tristan und Isolde*
1899	Emma sings *Lohengrin* at Windsor Castle, in the presence of Queen Victoria

1904	Emma makes her first recording in London
1911	Emma sings her farewell at Albert Hall; publishes her memoirs *Forty Years of Song*
1920	Emma is awarded a pension £100 year, owing to "difficult circumstances," by the British Government
1925	Emma is refused a request for a pension by both the Canadian and Québec governments; King George V awards her the title Dame Emma Albani
1930	Emma Albani dies and is buried in London